Destination Detectives

United Kingdom

North America

Europe

UNITED KINGDOM

Asia

Africa

South America

Australia

Rob Bowden

Raintree

Chicago, Illinois

Produced for Raintree Publishers by Discovery Books Ltd
Printed in China by South China Printing Company

11 10 09 08 07
10 9 8 7 6 5 4 3 2 1

Library of Congress Cataloging-in-Publication Data
Bowden, Rob.
  United Kingdom / Rob Bowden.
    p. cm. -- (Destination detectives)
  Includes bibliographical references and index.
  ISBN-13: 978-1-4109-2930-3 (lib. bdg.)
  ISBN-10: 1-4109-2930-2 (lib. bdg.)
  ISBN-13: 978-1-4109-2941-9 (pbk.)
  ISBN-10: 1-4109-2941-8 (pbk.)
  1. Great Britain--History--Juvenile literature. 2. Northern
Ireland--History--Juvenile literature. 3. Great Britain--Social
life and customs--Juvenile literature. 4. Northern Ireland--
Social life and customs--Juvenile literature. 5. Great Britain--
Geography--Juvenile literature. 6. Northern Ireland--
Geography--Juvenile literature. I. Title. II. Series.
  DA27.5B6845 2007
  941--dc22
                                    2005032921

This leveled text is a version of *Freestyle:
Destination Detectives: United Kingdom,* produced for
Raintree Publishers by White-Thomson Publishing Ltd.

Acknowledgments
Rob Bowden pp. 6 (Chris Fairclough Worldwide),
7 (Chris Fairclough Worldwide), 8-9 (Chris Fairclough
Worldwide), 9 (Chris Fairclough Worldwide), 12-13
(Chris Fairclough Worldwide), 20r, 21, 25, 26-27, 33, 34,
37 (Chris Fairclough Worldwide), 42 (Chris Fairclough
Worldwide); Getty Images pp. 16-17 (Matt Cardy),
23 (Scott Barbour), 26, 43; Photolibrary pp. 4
(Photolibrary.Com, Australia), 5l (Jon Arnold Images),
10 (The Travel Library Limited), 11 (Photolibrary.Com),
22 (Robin Smith), 24t (Index Stock Imagery), 26, 27
(Tony Bomford), 31 (Foodpix), 38 (Niall Benvie), 40
(Ruth Brown), 43; Topfoto pp. 5t, 14-15 (Gordon
Nicholson/Spectrum Colour Library), 24b (ESC), 30
(Gordon Davis), 35 (Photonews Service Ltd Old Bailey),
36 (WDS), 38-39 (Brandt); WTPix pp. 5m, 5b, 18-19,
20l, 28-29, 32, 40-41

Cover photograph of Big Ben and the Houses of Parliament
reproduced with permission of Photolibrary/Purestock.

Every effort has been made to contact copyright
holders of any material reproduced in this book.
Any omissions will be rectified in subsequent
printings if notice is given to the publishers.

The paper used to print this book comes from
sustainable resources.

Contents

Any words appearing in the text in bold, **like this,** are explained in the glossary. You can also look out for them in the Word Bank box at the bottom of each page.

Where in the World?

You wake up to an amazing noise. There are drums, whistles, and guitars. You step outside your hotel and follow the sound.

Round a corner you see hundreds of people. They are from all different backgrounds. Some are dancing. Some are dressed in fantastic costumes. It's a carnival. But where in the world are you?

Notting Hill

This picture (below) shows the Notting Hill Carnival. It is the biggest street carnival in Europe. The carnival takes place in west London every August.

Just then, a big red bus goes by. There is a poster for a show on the back of it. This reads "Now showing in London's West End."

You are in London (see map, page 7). This is the capital of the United Kingdom. A nearby voice says "Come and join the Notting Hill Carnival!"

In London, people of many different **cultures** live side by side. The carnival celebrates this.

▼

Find out later...

...why these people are chasing a ball of cheese.

...where you can see these famous landmarks.

...how the United Kingdom is reducing road traffic.

culture customs and beliefs of a particular group or country

A Varied Kingdom

You leave the carnival after a while. A few streets away, you find a café. There's a map of the United Kingdom on the wall here. It's covered with postcards and notes. You read them all.

Four countries in one

The United Kingdom is made up of four countries. They are England, Wales, Scotland, and Northern Ireland. The rest of Ireland is not part of the United Kingdom.

The United Kingdom at a glance

OFFICIAL NAME:
United Kingdom of Great Britain and Northern Ireland

POPULATION:
58.8 million

AREA:
94,248 square miles (244,101 square kilometers)

CAPITAL:
London

OFFICIAL LANGUAGE:
English

CURRENCY:
pound sterling (£)

Countries of the United Kingdom

Country	Area (sq. miles / sq. km)	Population (2001 census)
England	50,351 / 130,410	49.1 million
Scotland	30,421 / 78,789	5.1 million
Wales	8,015 / 20,758	2.9 million
N. Ireland	5,461 / 14,144	1.7 million

This is the Giant's Causeway in Northern Ireland. It is made up of thousands of columns of rock. They were created 60 million years ago. This happened when a volcano **erupted**.

Scotland and Wales are the most mountainous regions of the United Kingdom.

The United Kingdom has a long coastline. It is 7,723 miles (12,429 kilometers) long.

Orkney Islands

Shetland Islands

Hebrides

Scottish Highlands

NORTH ATLANTIC OCEAN

SCOTLAND

NORTH SEA

Edinburgh

Glasgow

NORTHERN IRELAND

Newcastle

The United Kingdom has many historic cities. These include London, Oxford, Edinburgh, and York.

Belfast

ENGLAND

York

IRISH SEA

Leeds

IRELAND

Liverpool

Manchester

Sheffield

Lincoln

Nottingham

Wales has its own language. Signs here are written in both Welsh and English.

WALES

Severn

Birmingham

Coventry

Cotswolds

Oxford

Colchester

London

Cardiff

Thames

Bath

Southampton

Brighton

Isle of Wight

Plymouth

N
W   E
S

English Channel

0   200 km
0   100 miles

CHANNEL ISLANDS

FRANCE

United Kingdom

A Historic Land

You want to know more about the history of the United Kingdom. You start by visiting Stonehenge. This is an ancient circle of standing stones. It is in southern England.

No one knows why the stones were put there. This might have been a place of worship. The oldest parts of Stonehenge were built over 5,000 years ago. Some of the stones are up to 30 feet (9 meters) high.

Stonehenge is made up of four stone circles. These circles stand one inside another. A wide ditch surrounds it.

➤

Roman Britain

In the year A.D. 43, Roman armies arrived in southern England. That was nearly 2,000 years ago. The Romans came from Europe. They ruled parts of the United Kingdom for almost 400 years.

The Romans built many important cities. London was one of them. They also built some of the first roads across England (see map, page 7).

➤ Hadrian's Wall separated Scotland from England in Roman times.

Hadrian's Wall

Hadrian was a Roman Emperor. He ordered a huge wall to be built between Scotland and England. The year was A.D. 122.

The wall was built to keep out the tribes who lived in Scotland. Hadrian's Wall was 73 miles (118 kilometers) long. You can still see parts of it today.

A revolution begins

You want to find out about more recent history. So you go to the Black Country. This is an area in central England. It is near the city of Birmingham (see map, page 7).

The Black Country was at the center of the **Industrial Revolution**. This was a period during the 1700s and 1800s. It took place about 150 to 250 years ago. Many new machines were invented. It was a time of great change in the ways that people worked.

(see map, page 7).

New invention

Iron is a metal. It has to be taken out of rock. In about 1700, people discovered a new way of producing iron. This meant that iron could be used for buildings. It could also be used for making new machinery.

This was the first iron bridge built in Europe. It opened in 1781. The Iron Bridge is in central England.

WORD BANK Industrial Revolution period during the 1700s and 1800s. This was a time of rapid improvements in industry.

All change

Hundreds of factories opened. The goods they made needed transporting. So new **ports** and railroads were built. Ports are places where ships can load and unload.

Some of the United Kingdom's largest cities began to grow. The Industrial Revolution helped make the country wealthy.

Age of Empire

Money from the Industrial Revolution made the United Kingdom more powerful. The United Kingdom took control of more countries. By 1900 it ruled almost a quarter of the world.

The British ruled India from 1757 to 1947. This picture shows British lords and ladies visiting an Indian prince.

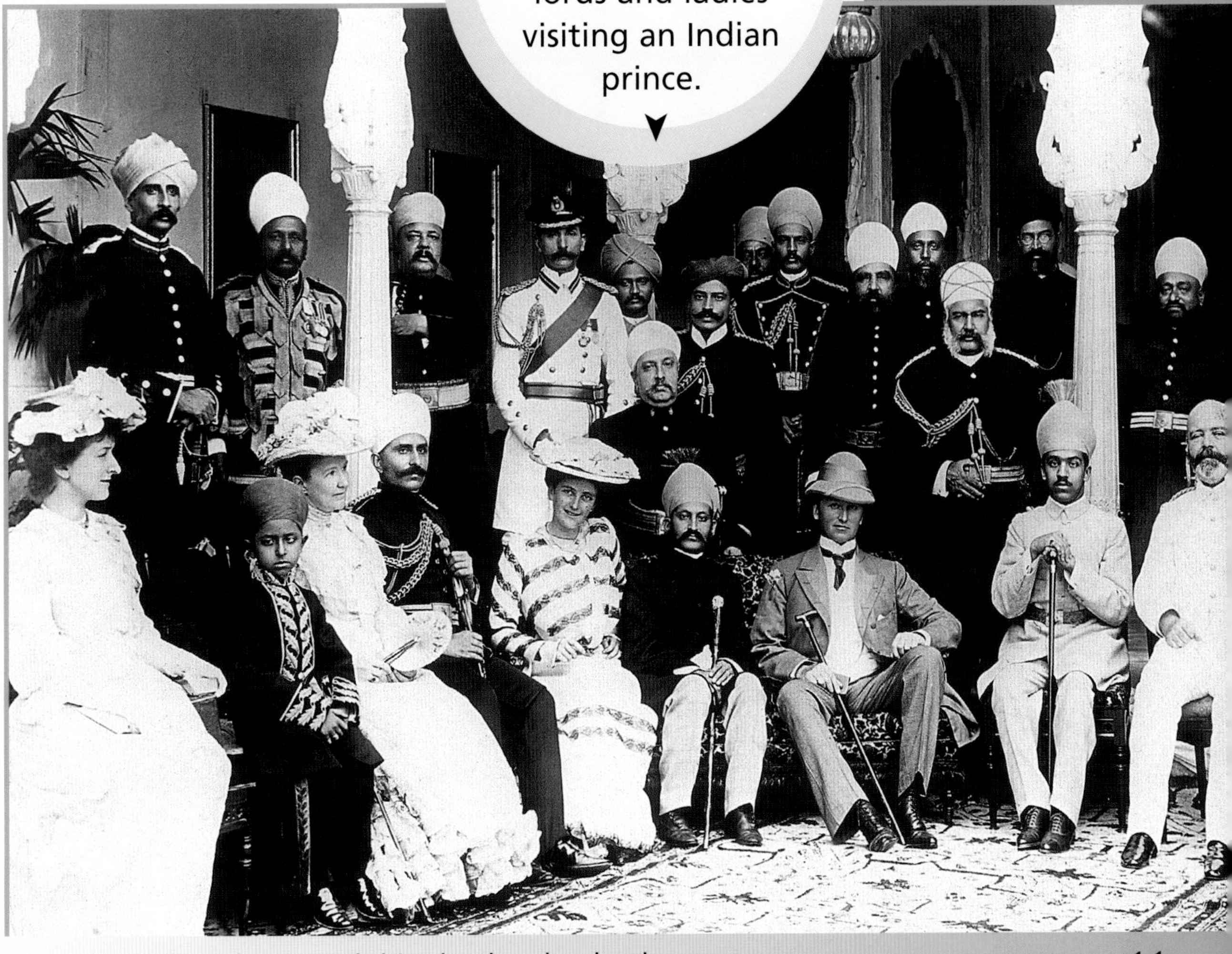

port place where boats and ships load and unload goods or passengers

Century of Change

You spend some time exploring the Black Country. But there's not much left of the old **industries** (types of businesses). Some of the industrial centers are now museums. So what happened?

The United Kingdom at war

The United Kingdom fought two world wars in the 1900s. The first was in 1914–1918. The second was in 1939–1945. Over 1.5 million British people were killed. The wars cost a lot of money. Industries suffered because of this.

This is the city of Coventry. The city was badly bombed in World War II. A modern cathedral stands next to the ruins of the old one.
➤

WORD BANK   industry type of work or business that produces or sells goods

Industries

Things got better in the 1950s and 1960s. There were new jobs for people. But industries began to fail again in the 1970s. Other countries could make goods for less money. So the United Kingdom stopped making them.

Coal mines shut down. **Shipyards** and other workplaces shut down. Thousands of people lost their jobs.

Women at war

Before World War II, most women did not have jobs. They did not work in offices or factories. Their work was in the home. Now over 40 percent of workers in the United Kingdom are women.

shipyard place where ships are built and repaired

Modern Manchester

How have all these changes affected the United Kingdom? You go to Manchester to find out. This is a major city.

Manchester still has lots of old industrial buildings. But most of them have been turned into stores or offices. Some are homes.

There are huge new shopping centers. There are also big entertainment centers. These are some of the United Kingdom's main **industries** today.

Ethnic groups in the United Kingdom

White – 92.1 percent

Asian – 4 percent

Black – 2 percent

Mixed – 1.2 percent

Other – 0.7 percent

Manchester has some striking modern buildings. This is the Urbis Centre. It is a museum about city life.

➤

They are known as **"service industries."** They provide people with a service instead of a product.

Building boom

In another part of Manchester, you see old houses being pulled down. There's a sign showing what will replace them. It shows new housing, stores, and offices.

This type of building work is happening everywhere. Construction is now one of the country's most important industries.

New arrivals

After World War II, the United Kingdom needed more workers. So the **government** invited people from other countries to move there. This is one reason why the United Kingdom now has large black and Asian populations.

service industries industries that provide services, such as banking, insurance, entertainment, and selling goods

City Life

Manchester is one of the United Kingdom's largest cities. It grew because of its **industries**. Other cities have grown for different reasons.

- London is the capital city. It is located on the Thames River. For hundreds of years, London has been an important **trade** center. *Trade* means "buying and selling" goods.

- Oxford is a center of learning. It has one of the oldest universities in the world.

- Belfast is the capital of Northern Ireland. It is an important **port** and **shipyard**.

Largest cities

The three largest cities in the United Kingdom are London, Birmingham, and Manchester.

- Over 7 million people live in London

- Birmingham has a population of more than 2,270,000

- More than 2,250,000 people live in Manchester.

WORD BANK   port place where boats and ships load and unload goods or passengers

• Edinburgh is the Scottish capital. It is home to a famous castle. The city hosts the world's largest arts festival.

• Birmingham is the United Kingdom's second-largest city. It was once the most important industrial city. Today it is a major center for entertainment. Conferences are held there, too.

• Cardiff is the Welsh capital. It used to be a busy port. Now it is an important business center. It has one of the United Kingdom's best sports stadiums.

You can look at the map on page 16 to see where all these cities are located.

People gather in Edinburgh for the famous arts festival.

shipyard place where ships are built and repaired

You are here!

London•

The Docklands

Canary Wharf (right) was built on London's old docks. It is a major business center. Canary Wharf is home to the country's tallest building. This is called Canada Tower.

London

London (see map on left) is by far the country's biggest city. It is the capital of the United Kingdom. You decide to go back there. You want to know more about life in the capital.

London has some very wealthy areas. Houses in these parts are very expensive. But close by are poorer housing areas. Many are run down and overcrowded.

Canada Tower

Canary Wharf is in East London. The area is now a mixture of offices and housing.

Spreading out

City housing is expensive. This is particularly true in London. Because of this, many people live on the edges of the city. Houses are cheaper there.

Commuting

Many people have to travel into the city center to work. They travel mostly by car, train, or bus. This is called **commuting**. Traffic gets very heavy at the beginning and end of the working day. Sometimes the transportation systems get clogged up.

2012 Olympics

In 2005 London was chosen to host the 2012 Summer Olympic Games. The games will be based in a poor area of East London. New buildings for the games will improve this area.

commute travel into a city from another area to get to work

Fun in London

All across London you see posters advertising shows and events. There is always so much to do in a city! You decide to make some notes about city life. You write a list of what's good and what's bad about city life.

On the tram

Several cities in the United Kingdom have started to use **streetcars** again. Streetcars are a type of train that runs through city streets (see picture above). They are helping to cut down road traffic and pollution.

London's West End is packed with theaters. They show world-famous plays and musicals.

WORD BANK   streetcar type of train that runs on rails through city streets

Benefits of city life

- Lots of jobs for people.
- Many different types of transportation.
- A chance to meet people from different backgrounds and countries.
- Plenty of restaurants.
- Plenty of theaters and museums.
- All types of stores and markets.

Problems of city life

- Heavy traffic clogs up the roads. It also causes **pollution**.
- Trains and buses can get overcrowded.
- It can be very expensive to live in big cities.
- In some parts there can be a lot of crime.

The Tube
"The Tube" is an underground subway system. There are 274 Tube stations in London.

Many cities have a "Chinatown." London has one. This is an area full of Chinese restaurants and stores.

➤

pollution release of harmful chemicals or waste into air, water, or soil

Education

Most universities and colleges are in cities or towns. There are 125 universities in the United Kingdom. To find out more, you visit Oxford. This is home to a famous university.

The University of Oxford began teaching in the 1100s. This was about 850 years ago. It is one of the world's oldest and best universities.

The boat race

Cambridge is the country's second-oldest university. Every year it has a boat race with Oxford University. This race takes place on the Thames River in London. Crowds of people come to watch.

Christ Church College is part of Oxford University. Thirteen British prime ministers (leaders) have attended this college. ➤

School

Children in the United Kingdom have to go to school between the ages of four and sixteen. They go to primary school until they are eleven years old. Then they go to secondary school until the age of sixteen. At the end of this period, they take examinations.

Some people stay at school for two more years. They study for more examinations. They have to do this if they want to go to college.

University numbers
There are 2.25 million university students in the United Kingdom.

In secondary schools, there are usually about 30 students in a class.

Life in the Countryside

There are some beautiful villages around Oxford. The area is known as the Cotswolds. This is a good place to find out about country life. (See map on page 7.)

Many villages in the United Kingdom are just a group of houses. Some have a church, a school, and a small grocery store. There may be a village green. This is a plot of grassy land. Villagers use it for sports or for special events.

On a roll!

The United Kingdom has some strange countryside traditions. One of these takes place at Cooper's Hill. This is in the Cotswolds.

People chase a large round cheese down a hill (above). The winner is the first to reach the bottom.

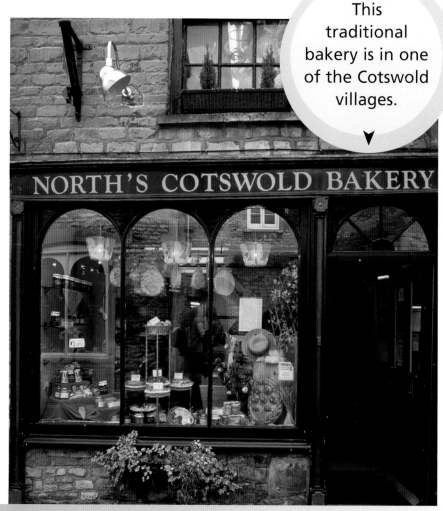

This traditional bakery is in one of the Cotswold villages.

WORD BANK   remote far away from other places or people

Remote villages

Some villages are far away from other towns. These **remote** villages may be many miles from a grocery store or post office. There are some villages in Scotland and Wales that are very remote.

The Plague Village

Eyam is a famous village in Derbyshire. In 1665 a village tailor brought some cloth to Eyam. There were fleas in the cloth. They carried the **plague**. This was a terrible disease. Within a year it killed more than half of the people in the village.

PLAGUE COTTAGE

Mary Hadfield, formerly Cooper, lived here with her two sons, Edward and Jonathan, her new husband, Alexander Hadfield and an employed hand George Viccars.

George Viccars, the first plague victim, died on 7th September 1665
Edward Cooper, aged 4 died on the 22nd September 1665
Jonathan Cooper, aged 12, died on the 2nd October 1665
Alexander Hadfield died on the 3rd August 1666
Mary alone survived, but lost 19 relatives.

This is the house in Eyam where George Viccars lived. He was the man who brought the plague to the village.

plague highly infectious disease

Farming

Farming is an important **industry** in the United Kingdom. Farms produce food for local needs. They also produce food for **export**. This food is for sale to other countries.

Part of eastern England has areas of low, flat land. This is ideal for large cereal and vegetable farms. Wales, northern England, and Scotland have lots of hilly regions. Sheep and other animals are farmed here. Southern England has a warmer **climate**. This is good for growing fruit. (See map on page 7.)

Countryside jobs

Some people in the countryside still do traditional jobs. The picture below shows a farrier. His job is to make and fit horseshoes.

Climate

Farming is affected by the weather. But weather in the United Kingdom is generally mild. It is rarely too hot or too cold.

There are four seasons. Summer is the warmest time of year. This lasts from June to August. Winter lasts from December to February. There can be snow then. The north and west of the country are usually the wettest and coolest places.

combine harvester

Machines are used for most farming work today. This **combine harvester** is gathering crops.

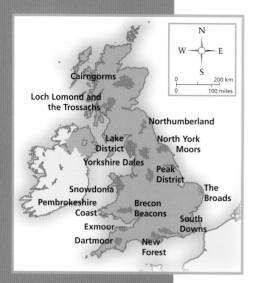

The Scottish Highlands

You want to see some wilder parts of the United Kingdom. So you travel north. You go to the Highlands of Scotland (see map, page 7).

This is a wonderful place for watching wildlife. It is home to red deer, otters, and golden eagles. Millions of seabirds live along the coastline. You can also see whales, dolphins, and seals here.

Going wild

About 10 percent of land in the United Kingdom is national parkland. National parks are specially protected areas. They are popular with walkers, cyclists, and climbers.

Wild beauty

The United Kingdom has other wilderness areas, too. They include:

- The mountains of Mourne—low-lying mountains in Northern Ireland.
- Snowdonia—a region of mountains and lakes in North Wales.
- Dartmoor and Exmoor—two **moorland** areas in southwest England. These are wide, open spaces known for their beauty. (See map, page 28.)

Top spot

The highest mountain in the United Kingdom is Ben Nevis. This is in the Scottish Highlands (see map, page 7). It is 4,406 feet (1,232 meters) high.

Crummock Water and Fells forms part of the Lake District. This is an area of northern England. It is now a national park.

moorland large area of open land with few trees

Eating and Drinking

Food in the United Kingdom often has a foreign flavor. But some regions have their own special foods. You can try some of them in Scotland.

Regional favorites

- Haggis—A Scottish dish made of a sheep's stomach. It is stuffed with oats and spices. It is also stuffed with minced offal. Offal is the inside parts of animals, such as the heart and liver.

Haggis is available in shops and restaurants all over Scotland.

- Black pudding—A dark-colored sausage. It is made mainly of pigs' blood. Black pudding is popular in northern parts of the United Kingdom.

- Laver bread—A seaweed and oatmeal cake. This is part of a traditional fried breakfast in Wales.

- Champ—A Northern Irish dish. Champ is made of potatoes fried in butter. Onions and cabbage are fried with them.

- Pork pie—A pastry case filled with chopped and spiced pork. Pork pies originally came from Melton Mowbray. This is in central England.

- Cornish pasty—Folded pastry filled with meat, potatoes, and other vegetables. The pasty was first made in Cornwall in southwest England.

Local markets

Farmers' markets (below) are good places to buy fresh food. These markets are popular across the United Kingdom. They sell special local foods. These include cheeses, sausages, and drinks.

Fast food

Asian food is especially popular in the United Kingdom. The city of Manchester has an area with about 50 Indian restaurants. This is known as the "Curry Mile." (See map, page 7.)

Traditional food

The most famous British meal is fish and chips. There are fish-and-chip shops in almost every town.

Traditional dinners of roast meat and vegetables are still popular. People often cook this type of meal on Sundays. They also cook them for special occasions.

People often enjoy eating fish and chips straight from the wrapping.

English tea

People in the United Kingdom love to have a cup of tea. But tea is not grown in the country. It first came to the United Kingdom from China in 1653. It quickly became the national drink.

Fast sailing boats used to rush the tea from China to London. They were called tea clippers. Most tea today comes from India and Africa.

This is the *Cutty Sark*. It is the last surviving tea clipper in the United Kingdom. It was built in 1869 to bring tea from China.

Culture and Religion

You've tasted some of the country's food. Now you look through a "What's On" guide. This lists some popular events.

- *Romeo and Juliet*—a new performance of a great play. It was written by William Shakespeare. He is one of England's most famous writers.

- Morris-dancing festival—Morris groups tour the country. They perform traditional folk dances.

Morris dancing is usually performed at country festivals.

- Welsh male voice choir concert—Wales is world-famous for its male voice choirs. They are made up entirely of men. Many of the songs they sing are in the Welsh language.

- Belfast Music Live—This is a music festival. Many local bands and musicians take part.

- Edinburgh Festival—This is the world's biggest arts festival. There is theater and comedy. There is also music and poetry. It features hundreds of different acts.

Festivals
Hundreds of festivals are held in the United Kingdom each year. There are festivals of the arts, poetry, and film. Others celebrate different types of music.

Glastonbury is a huge festival of music and performing arts. It is held on a farm in southwest England.

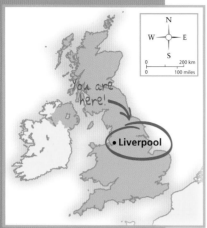
You are here!

• Liverpool

Religions

The main religion in the United Kingdom is **Christianity**. This religion is based on the teachings of Jesus Christ. But many other world religions are practiced in the larger cities.

You take a trip to Liverpool (see map on left). This is a good place to find out more.

Christianity

The center of Liverpool has two huge cathedrals. Liverpool Cathedral is the **Anglican** cathedral. Anglicanism is a form of Christianity. The Liverpool Metropolitan Cathedral is the

This is the modern Metropolitan Cathedral in Liverpool.

▶

WORD BANK   Anglican belonging to the Church of England. Anglicanism is a form of Christianity.

Roman Catholic cathedral. Roman Catholicism is another form of Christianity. This cathedral is famous for its tentlike shape.

All faiths

Liverpool, England, also has places of worship for Jews, Muslims, and others, too. There are many different places of worship in English cities. You won't find many of these places in Wales, Scotland, and Northern Ireland, though. Fewer non-Christians live in these areas.

Young Muslims study the Qur'an. This is their holy book. There are about 1.6 million Muslims in the United Kingdom today.

Roman Catholic belonging to the Roman Catholic Church. Roman Catholicism is a form of Christianity.

Travel and Tourism

The National Cycle Network

A group called Sustrans have built cycling paths around the country. They started building them in 1995. There are now more than 10,000 miles (16,000 kilometers) of cycling paths in the United Kingdom.

From Liverpool you can travel to almost anywhere in the United Kingdom. But what types of transportation are there?

Rail

Liverpool is connected to a national rail network. This covers England, Wales, and Scotland. Northern Ireland has its own rail network.

Roads

The United Kingdom's roads cover about 244,000 miles (392,400 kilometers).

WORD BANK   ferry boat for carrying passengers, goods, or vehicles across water

Expressways connect the cities and major towns. These expressways have up to four lanes of traffic in each direction. But they make up less than 1 percent of the road network.

Ferries

The United Kingdom has lots of **ferry** (boat) services. They connect the **mainland** with the islands. They also run between the different islands. Larger ferries operate services to other European countries. Some ferries operate from Liverpool.

Heathrow Airport
Heathrow Airport is in London. This is the busiest international airport in the world.

The CalMac ferry provides services to 22 islands off Scotland's west coast.

---

mainland main landmass of a country or continent

Tourist attractions

Some old forms of transportation are now tourist attractions. Steam railroads offer rides to tourists. People take boat trips on the canals and waterways. But what else attracts tourists to the United Kingdom?

Long history

The United Kingdom's long history draws visitors. Many enjoy visiting the historic buildings and castles. They come to see the ancient towns and cities. Tourists from all around the world come to see London's famous buildings.

▲

The Eden Project attracts nearly two million visitors a year.

The Eden Project

The world's largest greenhouse is in southwest England. It is part of the Eden Project. This is an education center. It is all about plants and the places where they grow.

Museums and stately homes

There are hundreds of museums and art galleries in the United Kingdom. The most popular ones are in London. But you'll find museums and art shows in lots of towns and villages, too.

Many of the United Kingdom's **stately homes** are open to the public. These are grand old houses. They belonged to important and wealthy families.

Landscape

The country's coastline attracts many visitors. People enjoy going to the beaches.

High-speed thrills

Adventure theme parks are among the United Kingdom's top tourist sites. They include:

- Alton Towers
- Blackpool Pleasure Beach
- Chessington World of Adventures.

London's Houses of Parliament is a top tourist attraction. The biggest bell inside the famous clock tower is known as Big Ben.

stately home grand house that has belonged to an important and wealthy family

Stay or Go?

From Liverpool, you travel to the south coast. You head for the popular seaside town of Brighton (see map, page 7). The airport is just a short journey from here. Will you stay or go home?

Island hopping

You could stay to explore some of the country's islands. West of Brighton is the Isle of Wight. This is famous for its boat races. The Isles of Scilly are off the southwest coast. They have beautiful white beaches and clear waters.

At the opposite end of the United Kingdom, there are the Shetland Islands (see map, page 7). People go there for the peace, beauty, and wildlife.

Brighton **Pier** opened in 1899. It has fun rides, games, and amusement arcades.

➤

WORD BANK   pier platform built on stilts that juts into the sea

Sport

You could take time to discover the many different sports of the United Kingdom. There are many traditional games. These include soccer, rugby, and cricket. There are also newer sports, such as surfing and mountain biking.

You could go to a big soccer match. There will be thousands of excited fans there. That would be an experience to remember!

Curling

Curling is an unusual Scottish sport. A player slides a stone across a sheet of ice. The aim is to get the stone close to the center of a target. Other team members sweep the ice in front of the stone. This helps the stone to slide along.

These chalk rocks are known as the Needles. They are off the coast of the Isle of Wight. A lighthouse stands on the farthest rock.

Find Out More

World Wide Web

If you want to find out more about the United Kingdom, you can search the Internet using key words such as these:

- United Kingdom
- London
- Scotland
- Wales
- Northern Ireland

You can also find your own key words by using words from this book. Try using a search directory such as www.google.com

Are there ways for a Destination Detective to find out more about the United Kingdom? Yes! Check out the books listed below:

Further reading

Blashfield, Jean F. *Enchantment of the World: England*. Danbury, Conn.: Children's Press, 2006.

Bowden, Rob. *The Changing Face of the United Kingdom*. Chicago: Raintree, 2005.

Kumari, Campbell. *United Kingdom in Pictures*. Minneapolis: Lerner Publications, 2004.

Heinrichs, Ann. *Enchantment of the World: Wales*. Danbury, Conn.: Children's Press, 2003.

Innes, Brian. *Nations of the World: United Kingdom*. Chicago: Raintree, 2001.

Minnis, Ivan. *The Troubled World: Northern Ireland*. Chicago: Heinemann Library, 2003.

Stein, R. Conrad. *Enchantment of the World: Scotland*. Danbury, Conn.: Children's Press, 2001.

Timeline

3000 B.C.
Stonehenge is constructed.

A.D. 43
Roman rule begins in parts of England.

A.D. 50
Londinium (London) is founded by the Romans.

A.D. 122
Hadrian's Wall is begun.

A.D. 365
Tribes from Germany begin to attack Roman Britain. These people are known as the Saxons.

A.D. 410
Roman rule in the United Kingdom ends.

A.D. 626
The city of Edinburgh is founded.

1066
Normans from France invade England and become rulers.

1249
The University of Oxford is founded.

1284
England gains control of Wales.

1297
Scottish Wars of Independence begin. These are a series of wars between England and Scotland.

1509
Henry VIII becomes King of England and Ireland.

1603
James VI of Scotland becomes James I of England, uniting the two kingdoms.

1700s
The **Industrial Revolution** begins in the United Kingdom.

1803
Richard Trevithick designs the first steam engine.

1914
The United Kingdom goes to war with Germany and its supporters. World War I ends in 1918.

1939
The United Kingdom is once again at war with Germany. World War II ends in 1945.

1952
Elizabeth II becomes queen of the United Kingdom.

1970s
Trouble breaks out in Northern Ireland, leading to years of conflict.

2005
London wins the campaign to host the 2012 Summer Olympic Games.

Industrial Revolution period during the 1700s and 1800s. This was a time of rapid improvements in industry.

UK: Facts and Figures

The flag of the United Kingdom is nicknamed the "Union Jack." It combines the crosses of the English, Irish, and Scottish flags.

People and places

- Population: 58.8 million (2001).
- Life expectancy at birth: men—76 years women—81 years.
- Highest point: Ben Nevis— 4,406 feet (1,343 meters).
- Coastline: 7,723 miles (12,429 kilometers).

Trade and industry

- Workforce: 29.8 million.
- Main **imports**: machinery, fuel, food products.
- Main **exports**: chemicals, food products, drinks.

Technology boom

- Cell phones: 49.7 million.
- Internet users: 25 million.
- Internet country code: .uk

WORD BANK   import products bought from other countries

Glossary

Anglican belonging to the Church of England. Anglicanism is a form of Christianity. In the United States the Anglican Church is called the Episcopal Church.

Christianity religion based on the teachings of Jesus Christ

climate normal weather conditions of an area

combine harvester machine that cuts down grain or cereal plants. It also separates the seeds from the stalks.

commute travel into a city from another area to get to work

culture customs and beliefs of a particular group or country

erupt to release lava and ash

ethnic groups people who come from a particular country, or who are descendents of people from that country

exports products sold to other countries

ferry boat for carrying passengers, goods, or vehicles across water

government group of people that makes laws and manages the country

imports products bought from other countries

Industrial Revolution period during the 1700s and 1800s. This was a time of rapid improvements in industry.

industry type of work or business that produces or sells goods

mainland main landmass of a country or continent

moorland large area of open land with few trees

pier platform built on stilts that juts into the sea

plague highly infectious disease

pollution release of harmful chemicals or waste into air, water, or soil

port place where boats and ships load and unload goods or passengers

remote far away from other places or people

Roman Catholic belonging to the Roman Catholic Church. Roman Catholicism is a form of Christianity.

service industries industries that provide services, such as banking, insurance, entertainment, and selling goods

shipyard place where ships are built and repaired

stately home grand house that has belonged to an important and wealthy family

streetcar type of train that runs on rails through city streets

trade business of buying and selling goods

Index